SIN

SIN

POEMS BY

Ai

BOSTON

HOUGHTON MIFFLIN
COMPANY

1986

Library of Congress Cataloging in Publication Data

Ai, date.

Sin.

I. Title.

PS3551.I2S5   1986   811'.54   85-21966
ISBN 0-395-37907-5
ISBN 0-395-37908-3 (pbk.)

Printed in the United States of America

V 10 9 8 7 6 5 4 3 2 1

The poems in this book have appeared in the following
magazines: *Agni Review:* "The Priest's Confession"; "The
Emigré." *The American Literary Review:* "Saint Anne's
Reel, 1870." *The American Voice:* "The Man with the
Saxophone." *Antaeus:* "Salome." *Bennington Review:* "Kri-
stallnacht," part 1; "The Death of Francisco Pizarro."
Cambridge University Poetry Magazine: "The Detective."
Callaloo: "Blue Suede Shoes." *Crazy Horse:* "More";
"Elegy"; "The Mother's Tale" (also reprinted in *Ms.*).
The Iowa Review: "Blue Suede Shoes"; "They Shall Not
Pass." *Ironwood:* "Two Brothers." *Michigan Quarterly
Review:* "The Testimony of J. Robert Oppenheimer." *Mis-
souri Review:* "The Journalist." *Paris Review:* "Conversa-
tion." *Poetry:* "Kristallnacht," parts 2–4. *The Seattle
Review:* "Immortality."

FOR GALWAY,

*who could see in me
when I was twenty,
the poet I hope to become.*

Many, many thanks to the National Endowment for the Arts for fellowships in 1985 and 1979–80, the CAPS program in New York, the Ingram Merrill Foundation, the PEN Emergency Fund for Writers (especially Christine Friedlander), and David Ignatow, without whose help I would not have survived to write these poems.

CONTENTS

SIN

TWO BROTHERS
A Fiction

1

Night tightens its noose.
You swim toward me out of sleep
like an eel,
as I put the glass canister
beside you on the bed.
Death, Bobby, hit me
like the flat of a hand.
Imagine you are made of crystal
and someone ice picks you
and you shatter,
all your cells coming
almost to despair
it is so good. Dallas. Dallas.
I turn toward the window,
then turn back to you.
Remember that Crayola drawing
of John-John's? —
the black smoke coming out the roof
of the White House
like curly black hair.
How Jackie spanked his hand
and drew him another
with angels lifting up?
Our own childhoods? —

days of ease and grace.
The good life sucking us deeper
and deeper in
toward its hot, liquid center,
where seasoned with the right diction,
schools, and politics
we would fry crisp and greaseless.
King for a day,
that's who I was.
I drove power,
the solid-gold Cadillac.
Go ahead, frown.
Tell me about the sin of pride
and I'll tell you
about the lie of forgiveness.
It wasn't Oswald killed me,
it was envy.

2

"I have this dream, Jack," you say.
"I'm at Arlington. It's twilight.
Thousands of funeral markers
rise from the ground
like dirty alabaster arms.
It's here, pilgrim,

2

they seem to say.
And then I'm in a room.
A man is counting green bills
sharp enough to cut,
while I pry the lid off a barrel
and peer down into it,
as if inside, there are dark green pickles
or steel-blue fish,
as if I were a boy
on a crowded street in Russia
with my hand around a coin
and the other in my brother's hand.
And while I scuff my shoe
and try to decide,
from far away I hear bugles, hoofbeats,
I see my brother's head
suddenly rise from his body
like a tiny pink ball
on a spout of dark red water,
clear past the rooftops
into the serene evening sky.
I am that boy, Jack,
dipping his hands
in the one standing barrel,
into water warm as blood,
with nothing to say to anybody,
except, 'My brother is the moon.' "

3

Riddles, I say,
lifting the lid off the canister.
I pull out a wet, gray mass,
stare at it, then put it back.
Some African tribes
eat the brains of their dead.
It brings them closer;
it kills them too.
But whatever it takes, Bobby, right?
I look out the window
at the deep rose welts of dawn,
streaking the sky's broad back,
then hand you the canister.
You lift out my brain.
When you bite down, I burn.
The air smells like creosote
and I stand before you,
my skin plump and pink,
my wounds healed.
I put my arms around you
and you disappear into me . . .

I stare at myself in the mirror:
Jack Kennedy,
thinner now, almost ascetic,

wearing the exhaust fumes of L.A.
like a sharkskin suit,
while the quarter moon
hangs from heaven,
a swing on a gold chain. My throne.
I step back and knot my tie.
Bobby, it's all a matter of showmanship.
You have to have the ability to entertain,
to stand like P. T. Barnum
in the enchanted center
of the public eye,
to drop your pants now and then
and have the crowd
cry for more,
to give it to them,
to take those encores,
till like the clown in Piaf's song
the show is all there is,
and the bravos, the bravos.
You give the people what they want, Bobby,
someone they can't help loving
like a father or an uncle,
someone who through his own magical fall
lifts them above the slime
of their daily lives.
Not God made man,
but man made God.

I step back to the mirror.
Break a leg, kid, I say to myself.
Give 'em a miracle.
Give 'em Hollywood.
Give 'em Saint Jack.

BLUE SUEDE SHOES
A Fiction

1

Heliotrope sprouts from your shoes, brother,
their purplish color going Chianti
at the beginning of evening,
while you sit on the concrete step.
You curse, stand up, and come toward me.
In the lamplight, I see your eyes,
the zigzags of bright red in them.
"Bill's shot up," you say.
"Remember how he walked
on the balls of his feet like a dancer,
him, a boxer and so graceful
in his blue suede shoes?
Jesus, he coulda stayed home, Joe,
he coulda had the world by the guts,
but he gets gunned,
he gets strips of paper
tumbling out of his pockets like confetti."

Is Bea here? I say
and start for the house.
"No," you say. "This splits us, Joe.
You got money, education, friends.
You understand. I'm talking about family
and you ain't it.

The dock is my brother."
Lou, I say and step closer,
once I was fifteen, celestial.
Mom and Pop called me sweetheart
and I played the piano in the parlor
on Sunday afternoons.
There was ice cream.
Your girl wore a braid down the center of her back.
The sun had a face and it was mine.
You loved me, you sonofabitch, everybody did.
In 1923, you could count the golden boys on your fingers
and I was one of them. Me, Joe McCarthy.
I gave up music for Justice,
divorce, and small-time litigation.
And you moved here to Cleveland —
baseball, hard work, beer halls,
days fishing Lake Erie,
more money than a man like you
could ever earn on a farm
and still not enough.
Pop died in bed in his own house
because of my money.
Share, he always said, *you share
what you have with your family
or you're nothing. You got nobody, boys.*
Will you cut me off now
like you did

when I could have helped my nephew,
when you hated the way he hung on to me,
the way he listened when I talked
like I was a wise man? Wasn't I?
I could already see a faint red haze
on the horizon;
a diamond-headed hammer
slamming down on the White House;
a sickle cutting through the legs
of every man, woman, and child in America.
You know what people tell me today,
they say, *You whistle the tune, Joe,
and we'll dance.*
But my own brother sits it out.

2

A man gets bitter, Lou,
he gets so bitter
he could vomit himself up.
It happened to Bill.
He wasn't young anymore.
He knew he'd had it
that night last July
lying on a canvas of his own blood.
After a few months, he ran numbers
and he was good at it, but he was scared.

His last pickup
he stood outside the colored church
and heard voices
and he started to shake.
He thought he'd come all apart,
that he couldn't muscle it anymore,
and he skimmed cream for the first time —
$10s, $20s.

You say you would have died in his place,
but I don't believe it.
You couldn't give up your whore on Thursdays
and Bea the other nights of the week,
the little extra that comes in off the dock.
You know what I mean.
The boys start ticking —
they put their hands in the right place
and the mouse runs down the clock.
It makes you hot,
but I just itch
and when I itch, I want to smash something.
I want to condemn and condemn,
to see people squirm,
but other times,
I just go off in a dream —
I hear the Mills Brothers

singing in the background,
Up a lazy river,
then the fog clears
and I'm standing at Stalin's grave
and he's lying in an open box.
I get down on top of him
and stomp him,
till I puncture him
and this stink rises up.
I nearly black out,
but I keep stomping,
till I can smell fried trout, coffee.
And Truman's standing up above me
with his hand out
and I wake up always with the same thought:
the Reds are my enemies.
Every time I'm sitting at that big table in D.C.
and so-and-so's taking the Fifth,
or crying, or naming names,
I'm stomping his soul.
I can look inside you, Lou,
just like I do those sonsofbitches.
You got a hammer up your ass,
a sickle in between your percale sheets?
Threaten me, you red-hearted bastard. Come on.
I'll bring you to heel.

3

Yesterday Bill comes by the hotel
and he sits on the bed, but he can't relax.
Uncle, he says, and points at his feet,
all I ever wanted was this pair of blue suede shoes,
and he takes out a pawn ticket,
turns it over in his hand, then he gets up,
and at the door holds it out to me
and says, *You keep it.*

Today I go down to the pawnshop
and this is what I get back — a .38.
Bill didn't even protect himself.
You have to understand what happened to him,
in a country like this,
the chances he had.

Remember Dorothy and the Yellow Brick Road?
There's no pot of gold at the end,
but we keep walking that road,
red-white-and-blue ears of corn
steaming in our minds: America,
the only thing between us
and the Red Tide.
But some of us are straw —
we burn up like Bill in the dawn's early light.

He didn't deserve to live.
This morning, when I heard he was dead,
I didn't feel anything.
I stood looking out the window at the lake
and I thought for a moment
the whole Seventh Fleet was sailing away beneath me,
flags waving, men on deck,
shining like bars of gold,
and there, on the bow of the last ship,
Dorothy stood waving up at me.
As she passed slowly under my window,
I spit on her.
She just stared at me,
as if she didn't understand.
But she did.
She gave up the Emerald City
for a memory.
I'd never do that, never.
I'm an American.
I shall not want.
There's nothing that doesn't belong to me.

THE PRISONER

1

Yesterday, the man who calls himself "Our Father"
made me crawl on smashed Coke bottles.
Today, I sleep. I think I sleep,
till someone beats on the door, with what? —
sticks, pans — but I don't move.
I'm used to it.
Still, when Our Father rushes into the room
and drags me out, I feel the old fear.
In the interrogation room,
he knocks me to the floor,
then sits on the side of his desk,
his arms folded, that sad look on his face
I know so well. He shakes his head slowly,
stops, and smiles.
"I've got something special today," he says,
"for a fucking whore of a terrorist bitch."
I want to say nothing,
knowing how denial angers him,
but I can't stop myself.
I'm not a terrorist, I say.
"That's not what I heard," he replies, standing up.
"Aren't you the friend of a friend of a friend
of a terrorist son of a bitch
who was heard two years ago to say
that someone ought to do something

about this government?"
I don't answer.
Already, I've begun to admit that it must be true.
"I lack just one thing," he says, "the name."
"I know you think you're innocent,
but you aren't.
Everyone is guilty."
He slaps me, then pushes one side of my face
toward the green glass.

2

I've been stung by a swarm of bees.
I'm eight. I'm running for the pond
on my uncle Oscar's farm.
Oscar, I cry. Our Father sighs deeply,
lifts me up, and sets me down in a chair.
"This Oscar," he says, handing me a notebook and pen,
"where can I find him?"
I don't hesitate, as I take the pen
and set it down
on the clean, blank paper.

3

Our Father lets me off
a block from my apartment.

He keeps the motor running,
but comes and leans
against the car beside me.
I try to guess the month. March, April? I say.
He tells me it's September,
to just take a look at the sky.
Then he tells me he was a prisoner once too.
I stare at his face,
the dry, sallow skin,
the long scar running from temple to chin.
"Oh this," he touches the scar gently,
"I got this playing soccer.
No, the real scars don't show.
You should know that.
You need time, though, to sort it all out.
I'm still a young man,
but sometimes I feel as old as the Bible.
But this is a celebration."
He takes a bottle of wine from the car
and we drink, while the stars glitter above us.
Done, he tosses the bottle into the street.
"Freedom," he says, "freedom is something you earn.
The others don't understand that, but we do."

CONVERSATION
For Robert Lowell

We smile at each other
and I lean back against the wicker couch.
How does it feel to be dead? I say.
You touch my knees with your blue fingers.
And when you open your mouth,
a ball of yellow light falls to the floor
and burns a hole through it.
Don't tell me, I say. I don't want to hear.
Did you ever, you start,
wear a certain kind of silk dress
and just by accident,
so inconsequential you barely notice it,
your fingers graze that dress
and you hear the sound of a knife cutting paper,
you see it too
and you realize how that image
is simply the extension of another image,
that your own life
is a chain of words
that one day will snap.
Words, you say, young girls in a circle, holding hands,
and beginning to rise heavenward
in their confirmation dresses,
like white helium balloons,
the wreaths of flowers on their heads spinning,
and above all that,

17

that's where I'm floating,
and that's what it's like
only ten times clearer,
ten times more horrible.
Could anyone alive survive it?

MORE
For James Wright

Last night, I dreamed of America.
It was prom night.
She lay down under the spinning globes
at the makeshift bandstand
in her worn-out dress
and too-high heels,
the gardenia
pinned at her waist
was brown and crumbling into itself.
What's it worth, she cried,
this land of Pilgrims' pride?
As much as love, I answered. More.
The globes spun.
I never won anything, I said,
I lost time and lovers, years,
but you, purple mountains,
you amber waves of grain, belong to me
as much as I do to you.
She sighed,
the band played,
the skin fell away from her bones.
Then the room went black
and I woke.
I want my life back,
the days of too much clarity,
the nights smelling of rage,

19

but it's gone.
If I could shift my body
that is too weak now,
I'd lie face down on this hospital bed,
this icy water called Ohio River.
I'd float past all the sad towns,
past all the dreamers onshore
with their hands out.
I'd hold on, I'd hold,
till the weight,
till the awful heaviness
tore from me,
sank to bottom and stayed.
Then I'd stand up
like Lazarus
and walk home across the water.

THE ÉMIGRÉ

I stare down from the terrace
at the firemen in their slickers,
black mice in black hats,
close my hand around some smoke,
then open it and that smoke is gone
like the Russia of my childhood.
When I was a girl,
my father worked for the Cheka.
One morning, he forced my mother outside
in her torn nightgown.
The apartment was filled with her scent —
ink, paper, fresh bread.
I was warm, full of potato latkes and milk.
I sang the song of the world revolution,
but that revolution betrayed my mother.
It's quiet now, as the fire trucks
pull out onto the asphalt sea
like tiny crimson arks,
as quiet as the apartment
when I stopped singing,
when my father said, *Come,*
your mother's safe.
I followed him down the steps,
but near bottom, I stopped.
He turned around
and held out his arms,
then I jumped.

I sit down at the word processor.
On the screen, a page
from the memoir I am writing.
Even now, I hear my father's voice
as he shouts at my mother.
She jerks her head toward me,
then raises her skirt and wipes her face.
I erase one word, another,
till the whole page is gone,
but I cannot erase that scene.
My mother is locked forever
in the Lubyanka inside me,
her dirty, bruised face
streaked with tears,
the handbills she'd printed
in that beautiful script of hers
torn and scattered about her on the floor
like mutilated black and yellow butterflies.

Now as I lean over the keys
with my eyes closed,
her face rises inside me,
a fat harvest moon
in a sky of India ink,
a face whose features are so clear,
so like my own
that I cannot deny them;

yet, I do deny them.
My life is mine. She's dead,
she died, she dies each time I write.
But no, she's alive.
She condemns me for leaving,
for bearing witness only in the dark.

I begin once more.
A scene fades in, out,
there are shouts from outside,
a door is flung back.
Mother *and* Father are taken from the room.
Father who worked for the Cheka,
murdered by the Cheka,
Mother who opposed it also murdered.
I go back to the window,
look up at the gray tarpaulin of sky
and see Father riding a red star
down from proletariat heaven
and farther out, Mother,
straddling her own renegade star,
gesturing and waving to me.
They want to teach me
to die for what I believe,
but I say disown the world, don't save it,
don't try. Live for what you believe.
Survive, survive another night.

23

But here they are, pressing their bloody faces
against the glass.
I slide the bolt back.
It's then our eyes meet,
my two brown, speckled marbles
and their sockets,
filled with the black, blinding light
of the universe.

THE MAN WITH THE SAXOPHONE

New York. Five A.M.
The sidewalks empty.
Only the steam
pouring from the manhole covers seems alive,
as I amble from shop window to shop window,
sometimes stopping to stare, sometimes not.
Last week's snow is brittle now
and unrecognizable as the soft, white hair
that bearded the face of the city.
I head farther down Fifth Avenue
toward the thirties,
my mind empty
like the Buddhists tell you is possible
if only you don't try.
If only I could
turn myself into a bird
like the shaman I was meant to be,
but I can't,
I'm earthbound
and solitude is my companion,
the only one you can count on.
Don't, don't try to tell me otherwise.
I've had it all and lost it
and I never want it back,
only give me this morning to keep,
the city asleep
and there on the corner of Thirty-fourth and Fifth,

the man with the saxophone,
his fingerless gloves caked with grime,
his face also,
the layers of clothes welded to his skin.
I set down my case,
he steps backward
to let me know I'm welcome,
and we stand a few minutes
in the silence so complete
I think I must be somewhere else, not here,
not in this city, this heartland of pure noise.
Then he puts the sax to his lips again
and I raise mine.
I suck the air up from my diaphragm
and bend over into the cold, golden reed,
waiting for the notes to come,
and when they do,
for that one moment,
I'm the unencumbered bird of my imagination,
rising only to fall back
toward concrete,
each note a black flower,
opening, mercifully opening
into the unforgiving new day.

THE GOOD SHEPHERD:
ATLANTA, 1981

I lift the boy's body
from the trunk,
set it down,
then push it over the embankment
with my foot.
I watch it roll
down into the river
and feel I'm rolling with it,
feel the first cold slap of the water,
wheeze and fall down on one knee.
So tired, so cold.
Lord, I need a new coat,
not polyester, but wool,
new and pure
like the little lamb
I killed tonight.
With my right hand,
that same hand that hits
with such force,
I push myself up gently.
I know what I'd like —
some hot cocoa by the heater.

Once home, I stand at the kitchen sink,
letting the water run
till it overflows the pot,

then I remember the blood
in the bathroom
and so upstairs.
I take cleanser,
begin to scrub
the tub, tiles, the toilet bowl,
then the bathroom.
Mop, vacuum, and dust rag.
Work, work for the joy of it,
for the black boys
who know too much,
but not enough to stay away,
and sometimes a girl, the girls too.
How their hands
grab at my ankles, my knees.
And don't I lead them
like a good shepherd?
I stand at the sink,
where the water is still
overflowing the pot,
turn off the faucet,
then heat the water and sit down.
After the last sweet mouthful of chocolate
burns its way down my throat,
I open the library book,
the one on mythology,
and begin to read.

Saturn, it says, devours his children.
Yes, it's true, I know it.
An ordinary man, though, a man like me
eats and is full.
Only God is never satisfied.

SALOME

I scissor the stem of the red carnation
and set it in a bowl of water.
It floats the way your head would,
if I cut it off.
But what if I tore you apart
for those afternoons
when I was fifteen
and so like a bird of paradise
slaughtered for its feathers.
Even my name suggested wings,
wicker cages, flight.
Come, sit on my lap, you said.
I felt as if I had flown there;
I was weightless.
You were forty and married.
That she was my mother never mattered.
She was a door that opened onto me.
The three of us blended into a kind of somnolence
and musk, the musk of Sundays. Sweat and sweetness.
That dried plum and licorice taste
always back of my tongue
and your tongue against my teeth,
then touching mine. How many times? —
I counted, but could never remember.
And when I thought we'd go on forever,
that nothing could stop us
as we fell endlessly from consciousness,

orders came: War in the north.
Your sword, the gold epaulets,
the uniform so brightly colored,
so unlike war, I thought.
And your horse; how you rode out the gate.
No, how that horse danced beneath you
toward the sound of cannon fire.
I could hear it, so many leagues away.
I could see you fall, your face scarlet,
the horse dancing on without you.
And at the same moment,
Mother sighed and turned clumsily in the hammock,
the Madeira in the thin-stemmed glass
spilled into the grass,
and I felt myself hardening to a brandy-colored wood,
my skin, a thousand strings drawn so taut
that when I walked to the house
I could hear music
tumbling like a waterfall of China silk
behind me.
I took your letter from my bodice.
Salome, I heard your voice,
little bird, fly. But I did not.
I untied the lilac ribbon at my breasts
and lay down on your bed.
After a while, I heard Mother's footsteps,
watched her walk to the window.

31

I closed my eyes
and when I opened them
the shadow of a sword passed through my throat
and Mother, dressed like a grenadier,
bent and kissed me on the lips.

THE MOTHER'S TALE

Once when I was young, Juanito,
there was a ballroom in Lima
where Hernán, your father,
danced with another woman
and I cut him across the cheek
with a pocketknife.
Oh, the pitch of the music sometimes,
the smoke and rustle of crinoline.
But what things to remember now
on your wedding day.
I pour a kettle of hot water
into the wooden tub where you are sitting.
I was young, free.
But Juanito, how free is a woman? —
born with Eve's sin between her legs,
and inside her,
Lucifer sits on a throne of abalone shells,
his staff with the head of John the Baptist
skewered on it.
And in judgment, son, in judgment he says
that women will bear the fruit of the tree
we wished so much to eat
and that fruit will devour us
generation by generation,

so my son,
you must beat Rosita often.

She must know the weight of a man's hand,
the bruises that are like the wounds of Christ.
Her blood that is black at the heart
must flow until it is as red and pure as His.
And she must be pregnant always
if not with child
then with the knowledge
that she is alive because of you.
That you can take her life
more easily than she creates it,
that suffering is her inheritance from you
and through you, from Christ,
who walked on his mother's body
to be the King of Heaven.

SAINT ANNE'S REEL, 1870

That morning, the preacher
held the Bible up to the window,
the sun shone through it,
and the word walked upright
on the other side —
you, a man in a blue wool suit,
with a woman's long hair
and girl's hands,
a pint bottle in your back pocket.
I stood beside my father
in my calico wedding dress
and thought
how I used to have pride in myself,
how I used to do things alone —
I raised the adobe wall
north side of this house,
I rubbed salve on my father's groin,
because he needed it
and I was unashamed.

After the wedding,
you made yourself a mother to me.
You sewed, cooked,
you hung the wash on Saturdays,
you danced between the bluish sheets
with clothespins in your mouth,
holding me by the waist, the hands,

then only with your grace.
No man could move like you,
and sometimes, I hid my face
against your shoulder,
as we reeled through ten years
to the hired man in our bed this morning,
me beside him.
Your tears.
And your forgiveness.
But I didn't want any of it.
I packed the buckboard
and loaded the boy, the girls,
the broken plates and skillet.
I drove the horses into the road.
You stood on the porch,
wearing the patched wool jacket,
a bottle to your lips,
your feet beginning to move easily
to the fiddle music in your head.
That music held us,
somehow still holds me,
but Jesse, nobody,
nobody can live between forgiveness
and a dance.

THE DEATH OF
FRANCISCO PIZARRO

Tonight Atahualpa's ghost
crowned me with cocoa leaves
and called me his little monkey.
But I knew who I was: Francisco Pizarro.
And when I died hours later,
I sailed away
down the green slide of Amazon to Galilee,
where Jesus was standing in a boat,
His brown hair like copper coins
strung on invisible wire.
Lord, I cried in my desolation,
to take a man like me —
and showed Him my hands,
hands that had held a continent,
and He plucked my head off my shoulders.
How small it looked as He turned it
'round and 'round in His surgeon's fingers.
I am thy Lord and thy God, He said,
with your last words, such bitter nuts
between my teeth.
Then He put my head in His mouth
and bit down hard.
My skull cracked like parchment
and my blood spilled from His mouth
onto His blue mantle.

See how you stain me, He said,
but I did not answer.
And He turned to the hard, rude men in the boat,
the ordinary men of all the ages of mankind,
who moaned and cried out in terror
and He said, *The kingdom of God is in you,*
but you must fight to keep it.
Even Pizarro has fallen in the battle.
And He opened His hands —
white feathers fell from them
and bones, so many bones
I could not count them all,
and He said,
Come, my lambs, come.
Who else can save you?

THE PRIEST'S CONFESSION

1

I didn't say mass this morning.
I stood in the bell tower
and watched Rosamund, the orphan,
chase butterflies, her laughter
rising, slamming into me,
while the almond scent of her body
wrapped around my neck like a noose.
Let me go, I told her once,
you'll have to let me go,
but she held on.
She was twelve.
She annoyed me,
lying in her little bed —
Tell me a story, Father.
Father, I can't sleep. I miss my mother.
Can I sleep with you?
I carried her into my room —
the crucifix, the bare white walls.
While she slept,
she threw the covers back.
Her cotton gown was wedged above her thighs.
I nearly touched her.
I prayed for deliverance, but none came.
Later, I broke my rosary.
The huge, black wooden beads

clattered to the floor
like ovoid marbles,
and I in my black robe,
a bead on God's own broken rosary,
also rolled there on the floor
in a kind of ecstasy.
I remembered how when I was six
Lizabeta, the witch, blessed me,
rocking in her ladder-back chair,
while I drank pig's blood
and ate it smeared across a slice of bread.
She said, *Eat, Emilio, eat.*
Hell is only as far as your next breath
and heaven unimaginably distant.
Gate after gate stands between you and God,
so why not meet the devil instead?
He at least has time for people.
When she died, the villagers
burned her house.

I lay my hand on the bell.
Sometimes when I ring this,
I feel I'll fragment,
then reassemble
and I'll be some other thing —
a club to beat,
a stick to heave at something:

between the act and the actor
there can be no separateness.
That is Gnostic. Heresy.
Lord, I crave things,
Rosamund's bird's nest of hair
barely covered by her drawers.
I want to know that you love me,
that the screams of men,
as loud as any trumpet,
have brought down the gates of stone
between us.

2

The next four years,
Rosamund's breasts grew
and grew in secret
like two evil thoughts.
I made her confess to me
and one night, she swooned,
she fell against me
and I laid her down.
I bent her legs this way and that.
I pressed my face between them
to smell "Our Lady's Roses"
and finally, I wanted to eat them.
I bit down, her hair was like thorns,

my mouth bled, but I didn't stop.
She was so quiet,
then suddenly she cried out
and sat up;
her face, a hazy flame,
moved closer and closer to mine,
until our lips touched.
I called her woman then
because I knew what it meant.
But I call you God, the Father,
and you're a stranger to me.

3

I pull the thick rope
from the rafter
and roll it up.
I thought I'd use this today,
that I'd kick off the needlepoint footstool
and swing out over the churchyard
as if it were the blue and weary Earth,
that as I flew out into space,
I'd lose my skin, my bones
to the sound of one bell
ringing in the empty sky.
Your voice, Lord.
Instead, I hear Rosamund's laughter,

42

sometimes her screams,
and behind them, my name,
calling from the roots of trees,
flowers, plants,
from the navel of Lucifer
from which all that is living
grows and ascends toward you,
a journey not home,
not back to the source of things,
but away from it,
toward a harsh, purifying light
that keeps nothing whole —
while my sweet, dark Kyries
became the wine of water
and I drank you.
I married you,
not with my imperfect body,
but with my perfect soul.
Yet, I know I'd have climbed
and climbed through the seven heavens
and found each empty.

I lean from the bell tower.
It's twilight;
smoke is beginning to gray the sky.
Rosamund has gone inside
to wait for me.

She's loosened her hair
and unbuttoned her blouse
the way I like,
set table,
and prayed,
as I do —
one more night.
Lamb stew, salty butter.
I'm the hard, black bread on the water.
Lord, come walk with me.

KRISTALLNACHT

1

I used to think
that dying is endless
like a fall from a high window.
But now that I am seventy,
I know it's more like a child
who is dying,
as I was in 1922,
a child who when he closes his eyes
sees ocean, miles of it,
a shore. And on that shore
dead children
all looking back over their shoulders.
And what those children see —
a child on a small rope bed,
his skin becoming
the electric blue of crushed lapis lazuli,
his head twisted back over a shoulder
death has whittled thin and sharp.
And angels on either side of the bed,
their wings not white, but gold,
their faces violet,
their hair iridescent —
speaking to the boy
or to anyone,

fluttery girlish voices
he can't make out.
What? What did you say? —
but the children on the shore understand.
They stretch out their hands to him.
The angels disappear
into a deep, deep pink
that must be smoke
and the boy falls back on the goose-down pillow,
thinking he'll fly into everlasting regret.

That's what dying is, I say,
and swing my thin legs
over the side of the bed
and sit up.
Or what I thought it was —
something too ugly
or too beautiful
to be kept secret.
I put out my cigarette.
Here I am, alive
in spite of myself
and not that boy
lying alone in a room
full of incense
and his own grating breath.

The nuns who cared for him,
having commended him
into the hands of Jesus Christ, our Lord,
having freed themselves
from one more mortal
and terrifying soul.
Someone who ascended a ladder of air
to an unearthly music,
his flesh vibrating and loosening
until he felt something grab him
around the waist and pull him back
toward the rope bed and candle light
to Sister Dominique
lifting the sheet to cover his face.
His breath coming suddenly, a divine wind,
and the sheet a sail,
carrying him across a river of stars.
Stars in his hair, his eyes, his mouth
and the nun's fingers to his lips,
as his lips pursed to kiss them,
but his teeth doing something else,
biting, biting till blood came
and everything so quiet:
Paul Mornais,
waking again in the world.

2

I was born in Cologne.
That word again: *Cologne.*
I let my mouth fill with it
as my mother did
when the pains began
and that word was black currant jam
on her tongue.
The sweetness filled her,
as the iron bed painted gold gleamed,
as the cottage began to spin,
as she herself spun
on the sharp end of nothingness,
until even her dark brown hair
had become blonde
and she became her own memory.
I wake beside the wicker basket
I slept in years ago.
Did it happen,
or did I dream it all, Mother? — you,
my German father,
killed before I was born,
the dove flying into my forehead
the moment I woke,
and pain as the beak broke through skin,
and then the smell of roses.

And petals falling to the floor
from the wound in my head,
as I bent to touch them
as they disappeared
into petals and late snow
beside your grave, Mother,
when I was twenty.
I was an orphan.
Why couldn't I accept that?
Didn't I have everything? —
that freedom from past
people had died for.

I stand back from my desk
and stare out the window.
I put my hands against the glass.
Cold. Snow. Winter in another country.
I blow on the glass and watch it fog up,
then I draw a cross on it
and circle it with my finger. The world.
One red line intersected by one black line.
Two roads,
and where they meet, a grave
and in that grave
bones wrapped in a coverlet of rose-red light —
you, Mother.
Just bones and a name and words:

Eulalie Mornais, who loved to dance.
Born 1882, died 1913.
God carry her to paradise
and dance there with her immortal soul.

3

The room was half in shadow,
half in light
and one white mum
arced toward me
from the turquoise enamel vase,
thirty-five years ago
in Paris in 1943
when a woman left me.
She was a woman like you,
fragile and thirty.
But I'm your psychiatrist.
I never touch you with my hands,
only with my voice, a pin,
I stick inside you
when you are drifting away
with your crayons and chocolate.
Tell me about your life, you say.
I look at my watch. Sunday at ten?
You stand and almost glide out the door.
What could I tell you? —

that in 1943, I was thirty,
a collaborator,
that Paris was mine
and I didn't want it.
That you make me feel as I did then —
frightened, mortal, and free.
I lift the phone and dial.
How are you? I say.
And you tell me you're afraid,
you feel like crying,
and I tell you
to color more diligently
and say good-by.
But what I wanted to say —
what was it really?
I close the curtains.
My wife knocks on the door. Lunch?
I remember lunch in Paris —
bread, Château Margaux, cheese, olives,
those nice full black ones
and machine guns across the street.
What did we French have to fear? —
sudden death, rape, torture,
or merely the passage of an ordinary day,
as I feared it
in my small room,
which the concierge kept so clean for me,

51

as she was sure my mother would.
If only I could have killed her cat;
it slept with me and I hated it —
the sexual clawing at the bedspread
when I was almost asleep,
that clawing like your presence day after day.
I walk to the door and open it ˙
and suddenly I am back in Paris in 1943.
I see my friend Klaus
dragging a young woman up the stairs.
He shoves her toward me.
For you, Paul, he says.
Untouched. For you.

4

The Jewess stood behind
the millinery shop window
and cursed us
and it seemed like the great wind
of the Bible was there with her
among the felt, the straw and feathers.
Her tongue was a snake.
Medusa, I thought,
and knew I'd turn to stone.
I had to stop her.

My voice and the voices
of the other good citizens of Berlin
that night in 1938
was a black wave filled with stars
that would wash over the Jews
and suspend them in atonement and broken glass.
I threw one rock and another
and realized I was alone —
glass was everywhere,
even in my hair,
and the Jewess lay at my feet,
her blood on my pants, my shirt.
I turned my face up
and glass fell in my eyes
and it felt like water, only water.
Paul, someone calls me, *it's raining.*
Come inside.

I walk back through the window
where the Jewess is still standing
and past her,
where a woman is bending
over the white wicker basket.
She looks up
and at that moment, I recognize you
and then you're gone, Mother,

and I'm standing alone,
beside the pond in the old convent yard,
where you are buried.
A woman is there on the water.
She lifts her arms
and the waves rise higher and higher,
but she does not drown.
I stretch out my hands.
Mother, strangle me.
Pretend I did not escape the rope bed,
but that you arrived as planned
in your velvet cloak the color of claret
and wrapped a silk cord around my neck
and pulled it tight.
Pretend I died for nothing
instead of living for it.

IMMORTALITY

I dreamed I was digging a grave
that kept filling with water.
The next day, you died.
I dressed you in a wool skirt
and jacket,
because you were always cold
and I had promised to do that much for you.
Then I took a potato to eat, went outside,
and started to dig.

I thought of the Great War;
the day we met.
You, thin as a spade handle,
wearing cotton in deep winter.
The sunset, a clot of dull red
floating in a bowl of cobalt blue,
as we lay on our backs in the mud,
my hand on your mons
and yours pushing at it,
pushing it away,
just like that.
And just like that, we parted.
Then one day you found me hoeing potatoes.
Let me help, you said,
and handed me a child
with bright red hair like yours.
I married you. We fought.
Blood sanctifies and blesses;

it binds.
Anna, where are you now? —
waltzing down a long mirrored corridor,
wrapped in glory that is red, bitter.

I toss a shovelful of dirt on your coffin.
It isn't that I hate you for giving it all up
with your poison.
But I wanted to do it —
to finally ease this hunger
to be holy in my devotion to you
and have you acknowledge it
the moment before I brought
the mallet down and set you free.
Life to you was yellow
like the vicar's daughter's braids,
it was morning-glories,
All Hallows' Eve,
your dead sister's baby teeth
for good luck.
But I wanted us to go on
day and night, without terror or hope.
I can't forgive your going.
I take the potato from my pocket.
One bite, then another,
if only this were all it took
to live forever.

ELEGY
For my cousin John, 1946–1967

Hundreds of flies
rise from my face
and I feel as if I'm flying.
But it's only a daydream.
I'm seventy-five,
in the veterans' hospital
and this isn't 1917.
On TV, Saigon is splitting apart
like a cheap Moroccan leather suitcase
and we are leaving it all behind;
our dirty, dirty laundry.
Maybe it's the right thing to do.
Maybe soldiers are reborn infinitely
to do each century's killing and mopping up.
We stand at attention in full dress.
A general rides by in an open car
and we cheer. How I cheered.
Here's to the trenches, the mud,
the bullet-riddled days and nights,
that one night in November 1917,
when I thought I was dead,
when I felt myself rising
straight for the moon's green, cheesy heart.
But I wasn't dead,
I was on a troop ship in the English Channel
twenty-seven years later
and nothing had changed.

Last night, I dreamed about my mother.
She was pregnant with me
and I was also there with her
as a young man.
I wanted to end it inside her womb
with my bayonet.
And somehow, I cut my way to the child.
I took him by the feet
and flung him high
over a smoky black rainbow.

2

Suddenly, my body jerks forward, then back
and just as suddenly,
the TV screen darkens
and the voices of the journalists fade,
then hang in the air like whispers,
as the orderly takes hold of my wheelchair.
When we move down the hallway,
small, almond-eyed people
cheer as I roll by.
I recognize them all:
that one was with me in the trenches,
that one in the concentration camp,
and that vapor there from Nagasaki.
The orderly lifts me into bed

58

and folds the mended blanket across my chest.
Imagining things, I say to him.
Well, what if I am? —
just lower the coffin.
Let those clods of earth come down
like a hundred blows.
You say never you, never,
but when it's your turn,
you'll pack your sweet dreams
in your old kit bag and go.
And on that true last day,
you and I will rise toward heaven
like two great brass notes
from Gabriel's horn.
We'll shout, *Hallelujah,*
the war is over.
We'll shout the gates
of heaven down.

THEY SHALL NOT PASS

Above me, the sky is all Atlantic
and I taste vinegar, salt,
and those hot yellow peppers
Natividad used to eat
with tamales and beer.
And the sweat above her lip —
I can taste that too.
And I have to remind myself
why I left Mexico,
why I'm dying here in Madrid
when I should be standing,
thumbs hooked in my belt loops,
a Lucky Strike caught in the corner of my mouth.

I was a Wobbly like my father
and like him, I always bought two drinks:
one for myself and one for the ghost
of universal brotherhood,
with his tattered suitcase, checkered tie,
and a thirst for handshakes and hammers,
always leaning at the bar when I'd arrive,
with his *Joe, buy me a drink, just one more.*
He was in Vera Cruz the night I left,
he stood on the deck with me before I sailed,
squinting at the dock, pointing out the ones
who were his,

while I stood there, empty of everything
but what I believed:
that your brother was your brother
and you had to spare a dime,
that when you went down,
the next man would stand up,
hand in his pocket,
that there were angels
who walked among the honored dead
carrying red sickles,
that Joe Stalin sat like Ole King Cole
top of the world
and I'd sit next to him someday
with the back pay of a thousand years
in my own hands.
I had a heart like a goddamn sponge.
You could fill me
with slogans, with songs and marches,
with dead men —
like Sunshine.

He was next to me
when he split up the middle,
out of luck, out of dimes;
when there was terror no one told me existed:
betrayers, idealists — hysterical and uneven fighters.

Only this: They shall not pass.
I said it over and over to myself
as we defended the University of Madrid,
even as I took this slow glide down,
my blood like thick bolts of cloth,
hitting the ground as I fell,
while the layers of ice and ash
floated down from kingdom come.

A chrome ship slides across the sky's smooth surface
and Franco himself lifts the Stars and Stripes sail.
My whole face is numb.
I wanted to hit the coast of Spain
like a fist ramming an old man's belly,
but instead found what's-his-name
in the first bar I stepped into,
wearing a Saint Patrick's Day smile:
Cold sober, Joe, he said, and he spat on the sawdust floor.
I'm my own man, first time in years.
You should try it.
Then he told me
a man can kill without hate,
that that's how it's done,
that Jesus Christ is the bullet
that makes everything right.
But it doesn't matter
now that the glorious perfumed air

is filled with butterflies
which have men's faces, men's feet,
now that the cocoon of flesh
that held me splits apart
and I step left, right, left,
and what's-his-name swaggers head of the line
and his voice floats over us
like the Holy Ghost:
Victory, friends, brothers;
as we march
all in a row
into the motionless sea.

THE TESTIMONY OF
J. ROBERT OPPENHEIMER
A Fiction

When I attained enlightenment,
I threw off the night like an old skin.
My eyes filled with light
and I fell to the ground.
I lay in Los Alamos,
while at the same time,
I fell
toward Hiroshima,
faster and faster,
till the earth,
till the morning
slipped away beneath me.
Some say when I hit
there was an explosion,
a searing wind that swept the dead before it,
but there was only silence,
only the soothing baby-blue morning
rocking me in its cradle of cumulus cloud,
only rest.
There beyond the blur of mortality,
the roots of the trees of Life and Death,
the trees William Blake called Art and Science,
joined in a kind of Gordian knot
even Alexander couldn't cut.

To me, the ideological high wire
is for fools to balance on with their illusions.
It is better to leap into the void.
Isn't that what we all want anyway? —
to eliminate all pretense
till like the oppressed who in the end
identifies with the oppressor,
we accept the worst in ourselves
and are set free.

In high school, they told me
all scientists
start from the hypothesis "what if"
and it's true.
What we as a brotherhood lack in imagination
we make up for with curiosity.
I was always motivated
by a ferocious need to know.
Can you tell me, gentlemen,
that you don't want it too? —
the public collapse,
the big fall smooth as honey down a throat.
Anything that gets you closer
to what you are.
Oh, to be born again and again
from that dark, metal womb,

the sweet, intoxicating smell of decay
the imminent dead give off
rising to embrace me.

But I could say anything, couldn't I?
Like a bed we make and unmake at whim,
the truth is always changing,
always shaped by the latest
collective urge to destroy.
So I sit here,
gnawed down by the teeth
of my nightmares.
My soul, a wound that will not heal.
All I know is that urge,
the pure, sibylline intensity of it.
Now, here at parade's end
all that matters:
our military in readiness,
our private citizens
in a constant frenzy of patriotism
and jingoistic pride,
our enemies endless,
our need to defend infinite.
Good soldiers,
we do not regret or mourn,
but pick up the guns of our fallen.

Like characters in the funny papers,
under the heading
"Further Adventures of the Lost Tribe,"
we march past the third eye of History,
as it rocks back and forth
in its hammock of stars.
We strip away the tattered fabric
of the universe
to the juicy, dark meat,
the nothing beyond time.
We tear ourselves down atom by atom,
till electron and positron,
we become our own transcendent annihilation.

THE DETECTIVE

I lie on my daughter's body
to hold her in the earth,
but she won't stay;
she rises, lifting me with her,
as if she were air
and not some remnant
of failed reeducation
in a Cambodian mass grave.
We rise, till I wake.
I sit up, turn on the lamp,
and stare at the photo of the girl
who died yesterday,
at her Vietnamese mother
and her American father.
Jewel van duc Thompson,
murdered in Springfield, Ohio,
in her eighteenth year,
gone the day she was born
like in the cartoons,
when somebody rolls up the road
that stretches into the horizon
and the TV screen goes black . . .

Go home, Captain,
the cop said yesterday,
as he gripped my hand

and hauled himself
up from the ditch
where they'd found her
like Persephone
climbing from the underworld
one more time,
his eyes bright,
the hunger for life
and a good time
riding his back like a jockey.
Death is a vacation, I answered.
Then my hand was free
and I could see
how she was thrown
from the highway
down the embankment.
Where were Art and Rationality
when it counted? I thought —
always around the corner
from somebody else's street.
Even the ice cream man
never, ever made your block,
though you could hear the bells,
though you could feel the chill
like a shock
those hot days

when your company beat the bushes,
when you bit into death's chocolate-covered center
and froze . . .

I turn off the lamp
and lie still in the dark.
Somewhere in time, it is 1968.
I am bending over a wounded man
with my knife.
My company calls me the Angel of Mercy.
I don't remember yesterday
and there is no tomorrow.
There is only the moment
the knife descends
from the equatorial dark.
Only a step
across the Cambodian border
from Vietnam
to search and destroy the enemy,
but it is just a short time
till the enemy discovers me
and I would die,
but for the woman
who takes me to the border,
who crosses with me from the underworld
back to the underworld.

I open the curtain.
Outside, the early morning
is spinning, gathering speed,
and moving down the street
like a whirlwind.
I pull the curtain shut again
and switch on my tape
of the murderer's confession,
hear the faint, raspy voice
playing and replaying itself.
It was Saturday night.
She stood alone at the bus stop.
When she took the first step
toward my car,
I dropped the key once, twice.
She smiled, she picked it up.
I lie back on the bed,
while the voice
wears itself out.
Yes, I think,
you live for a while.
You get tired.
You walk the road into the interior
and never come back.
You disappear
the way the woman

and your child disappear
into Cambodia
in the pink light of dawn,
early April 1975.
You say you'll go back,
but you never do.
Springfield, Phnom Penh.
So many thousands of miles
between a lie and the truth.
No, just a step.
The murderer's voice rises,
becomes shrill.
Man, he says, *is it wrong
to do what is necessary?*
I switch off the tape.
Each time I sit down,
I think I won't get up again;
I sink through the bed, the floor,
and out the other side of the Earth.
There my daughter denounces me.
She turns me back
at the muddy border of forgiveness.
I get up, dress quickly,
then open the curtain wide.

At the door,
I put my hand on the knob, hesitate,

then step out into sunlight.
I get into the car,
lift the key to the ignition,
drop it.
My hand is shaking.
I look into the back seat.
The Twentieth Century is there,
wearing a necklace of grenades
that glitters against its black skin.
I stare, see the pins
have all been pulled.
Drive, says the voice.
I turn to the wheel,
imagine the explosions,
house after house
disintegrating in flames,
but all is silent.
People go on with their lives
on this day that is one hundred years long,
on this sad red balloon of a planet,
the air escaping from it
like the hot, sour breath of a child.

THE JOURNALIST

1

In the old photograph,
I'm holding my nose
and my friend Stutz
has a finger down his throat.
We're sixteen, in Cedar Falls.
It's all still a joke.
In my mind, I'm back there.
The woman who used me
like a dirty rag is gone
in a red convertible.
The top is down.
She sits beside the Greek
from out of town,
his hair slicked down
with bergamot.
I don't care, I do care
that she cruises the streets
of Little America without me.
I take a last drag off my Lucky,
pull my cap low,
and take the old road to the fairground.
I'm sixteen. What do I know
about love and passion, I think,
as I watch the circus set up,
watch as the elephants pitch and sway,

heads and trunks swinging wildly.
When the yellow leaves stir
and spin around me,
I walk back to the river
and skim stones
across the clear, gold water
of early evening,
till the 7:18 whistle blows.
Then as if on command,
I start running from childhood,
from the hometown
that keeps me a boy
when I want to be a man.
Manhood, a dream, an illusion, I think,
as I lay down the photograph
and stand still in the anemic glow
of the darkroom lights,
my body giving off the formaldehyde smell
of the unknown.

2

In Vietnam in 1966,
I stood among the gathering crowd,
as the Buddhist nun
doused her robe with gasoline.
As an American, I couldn't understand

and as I stood there,
I imagined myself
moving through the crowd
to stop her, but I didn't.
I held my camera in position.
Then it happened so quickly —
her assistant stepped forward
with a match.
Flames rose up the nun's robe
and covered her face,
then her charred body
slowly fell to the ground.
That year in Vietnam,
I threw my life in the air
like a silver baton.
I could catch it with my eyes closed.
Till one night,
it sailed into black space like a wish
and disappeared.
Or was it me who vanished,
sucking the hard rock candy
of the future,
sure that a man's life is art,
that mine had to be?
But tonight, I'm fifty-three.
I've drunk my way to the bottom
of that river of my youth

and I'm lying there
like a fat carp,
belly-down in the muck.
And nothing, not the blonde,
the red car,
or the smell of new money,
can get me up again.

I lay out the photographs of the nun.
I remember how her assistant
spoke to the crowd,
how no one acknowledged her,
how we stood another two or three minutes,
till I put my hand in my pocket,
brought out the matchbook,
and threw it to the nun's side.
I stare at the last photograph —
the nun's heart that would not burn,
the assistant, her hand stretched toward me
with the matchbook in it.
What is left out? —
a man, me, stepping forward,
tearing off a match, striking it
and touching it to the heart.
I throw the photographs
in the metal wastebasket,
then take the nun's heart

from the glass container of formaldehyde.
I light a match.
Still the heart won't burn.
I put the fire out,
close my eyes
and see myself running,
holding a lump
wrapped in a handkerchief.
I think someone will stop me
or try to, but no one does.
I open my eyes,
take the heart,
and hold it against my own.
When I was sixteen,
I was the dutiful son.
I washed my hands,
helped my mother set the table,
got my hair cut, my shoes shined.
I tipped the black man
I called "boy" a dime.
I didn't excel,
but I knew I could be heroic
if I had to.
I'd set the sharp end
of the compass
down on blank paper
and with the pencil end

I was drawing the circle
that would contain me —
everything I wanted,
everything I'd settle for.
Life and all its imitations.
That day in Hue,
I had the chance to step
from the circle
and I took it.
But when I turned back,
everything inside it was burning.
My past was gone. I was gone.
But the boy was still there.
He watched the flames take the nun.
He took her heart. He was running.
I was bound, he said to himself, *I'm free.*
But it was a lie.

I put the heart back in the container,
hear the heavy footsteps
of my wife, the blonde,
who is gray now,
who is clumping up the stairs
in her rubber boots
like some female Santa Claus.
In the heavy canvas bag
slung over her shoulder —

all the smashed toys of my life.
Wait, I say, as I stand
with my shoulder against the door.
Wait. You haven't heard
the best part yet —
A boy is running away from home.
He's lost his cap.
He's wearing the icy wind
like an overcoat.
He can't go back. He won't go back.
He never left.

DATE DUE

9/4/95	Nichols PL		
6/24/96	EA		
JUN 0 6 2005			